A Note to Parents

Read to your child...

★ Reading aloud is one of the best ways to develop your child's love of reading. Older readers still love to hear stories.

★ Enthusiasm is contagious. Read with feeling. Show your child that reading is fun.

★ Take time to answer questions your child may have about the story. Linger over pages that interest your child.

...and your child will read to you.

★ Do not correct every word your child misreads. Say, "Does that make sense? Let's try it again."

★ Praise your child as he progresses. Your encouraging words will build his confidence.

You can help your Level 2 reader.

★ Keep the reading experience interactive. Read part of a sentence, then ask your child to add the missing word.

★ Read the first part of a story, then ask your child, "What's going to happen next?"

★ Give clues to new words. Say, "This word begins with *b* and ends in *ake*, like *rake, take, lake*."

★ Ask your child to retell the story using her own words.

★ Use the five *W*s: WHO is the story about? WHAT happens? WHERE and WHEN does the story take place? WHY does it turn out the way it does?

Most of all, enjoy your reading time together!

Photo credits: pages 6-7, 8-9, 11, 12 © Bettmann/CORBIS; page 31 © Action Sports
Photography, Inc.; pages 5, 14, 16-17, 18, 22-23, 28-29 CIA Stock Photography, Inc.; title page,
inset page 9, inset page 17, page 19, 20, 21, 24-25, 26, 27, inset page 24, inset page 29 Sherryl
Creekmore/NASCAR; inset page 7 © 2003 Motorsports Images and Archives. All rights
reserved. Used with permission.

Library of Congress Cataloging-in-Publication Data

Kelley, K. C.
Champions of NASCAR/by K.C. Kelley.
   p. cm. – (All-star readers. 2)
ISBN 13: 978-0-7944-0757-5
ISBN 10: 0-7944-0757-9
1. NASCAR (Association)–Miscellanea–Juvenile literature. 2. Stock car drivers–United States–
Miscellanea–Juvenile literature. I. Title. II. Series: All-star readers. Level 2.

   GV1029.9.S74K44 2005 796.72–dc22   2004065054

Champions!
of NASCAR

by K.C. Kelley

All-Star Readers™

Reader's Digest Children's Books™
Pleasantville, New York • Montréal, Québec

At the end of every NASCAR race, there's a winner. The winner is the driver who crosses the finish line first.

At the end of each NASCAR season, there is a champion. The champ is the driver who finishes first in a series of races called "The Chase for the NASCAR NEXTEL Cup." Winning a championship is the goal of every NASCAR driver.

NASCAR was born in 1948. In those days, many drivers drove their family cars in races! Tracks were often made of dirt or even beach sand.

One of NASCAR's early stars was Lee Petty. He won the championship in 1958 and 1959. His son, Richard, would become an even bigger race car star!

Richard Petty grew up around cars. When he was old enough, Richard started racing. He soon became the fastest driver on the track!

He won his first NASCAR title in 1964. In 1967, he won a record 27 races. By the time he quit NASCAR racing in 1992, he had won 200 races and seven championships. No NASCAR driver has won more races than Richard "The King" Petty.

Cale Yarborough grew up in South Carolina. He knew he wanted to be a racer even when he was a kid. He tried to drive in a NASCAR race when he was only 16! He got caught, but he came back a few years later—ready to race!

In 1976 he won his first championship. He won again the next two years. Cale is the only driver ever to win three straight NASCAR titles!

11

Race fans today know Darrell Waltrip as a popular NASCAR announcer. Before he started on TV, he was a three-time NASCAR NEXTEL Cup Series champion.

Darrell started driving in NASCAR in 1972. He won a total of 84 races. He is tied for third place for all-time NASCAR wins. Darrell won his first NASCAR championship in 1981. He won two more in the 1980s. Then he traded in his helmet for a microphone.

Richard Petty won a total of seven championships. So did Dale Earnhardt. Like Richard, Dale was the son of a former NASCAR star, Ralph Earnhardt, who raced in the 1950s.

Dale began racing in 1975. In 1980 he won the first of his seven championships. Dale's number 3 car was usually painted black. He was known as the "Man in Black."

In NASCAR, many families have enjoyed racing success. Only one set of brothers has each won a championship trophy.

Terry and Bobby Labonte grew up in Texas, racing in anything they

could drive. Both moved on to NASCAR racing. In 1984, Terry became the first champ in the family. He added another title in 1996. In 2000, it was Bobby's turn. He was the NASCAR NEXTEL Cup Series champion that year.

Bobby and Terry Labonte

Bill Elliott has two nicknames. One is "Awesome Bill from Dawsonville." The other is "Million Dollar Bill." In 1985, Bill won a million-dollar prize for winning three special races.

You could also call Bill "The Fastest Driver Ever." In 1987, he set a record by driving his car more than 212 miles per hour! You can also call him "Champ." In 1988, he won the NASCAR NEXTEL Cup Series Championship.

Most NASCAR stars take years to reach the top. Some are stars from the first time they hit the track. Jeff Gordon was one of those young stars. He won his first championship in 1995, his third season. He was just 23 years old.

Jeff won three more titles before he turned 30 years old! Only Richard Petty and Dale Earnhardt Sr. have won more titles than Jeff. However, Jeff is not done. Now he's a star driver, racing against today's young drivers!

Dale Jarrett is another NASCAR veteran. Like many drivers, he is from North Carolina. Dale's dad was a NASCAR champ. Ned Jarrett won it all in 1961 and 1965.

Dale started racing in 1984. He won some races, but never took the top spot. He was patient and kept learning and trying. Finally in 1999, he became the NASCAR champ. Like father, like son…again.

Indiana-born Tony Stewart began his career racing smaller sports cars. Soon he began driving in NASCAR races. In 1999, he was the Raybestos Rookie of the Year.

Tony's 2002 season didn't start off well. He finished last in the Daytona 500. But he never gave up. He went on to finish in the top five in 15 races. That earned Tony another trophy—the one for the NASCAR NEXTEL Cup Series championship.

When Matt Kenseth was 13 years old, his father bought a race car. At first, Matt just worked on the car. At age 16, he began racing in it.

Matt built his career step by step. He was the 2000 Raybestos Rookie of the Year. In 2002, he won five races. Then in 2003, he won NASCAR's biggest prize— the championship.

In 2004, NASCAR started a new way to find the champ. After 26 races, the top 10 drivers enter the Chase for the NASCAR NEXTEL Cup.

Kurt Busch won the first race of the Chase, the Sylvania 300 in New Hampshire. With that win, he jumped from seventh to second place in the Chase standings. Could Kurt reach the top?

Kurt moved to the top spot two weeks later. He held on tightly for race after exciting race. At the final race in Miami, he finished fifth. It was very exciting. At one point, Kurt's team had to replace a tire that had fallen off his car!

In the end, Kurt became the NASCAR NEXTEL Cup champion by only eight points over Jimmie Johnson. It was the closest finish in NASCAR history!